ARCHITECTURE ASIA

Journal of the Architects Regional Council Asia (ARCASIA)

CONTENTS

EDITORIAL

ARCASIA Awards for Architecture (AAA) is an annual award instituted by the Architects Regional Council Asia (ARCASIA) to encourage and recognize exemplary works produced by architects working in Asia, as part of ARCASIA's endeavors to raise the standard of the built environment throughout Asia, celebrate the Asian spirit, and enhance the awareness of the role of architects in the socio-economic and cultural life of Asian countries.

The ARCASIA Awards for Architecture 2022 (AAA 2022) was launched on March 15, 2022, on the ARCASIA and ARCASIA Forum 21 websites. The award committee was made up of Ar. Batjav Batkhuyag, Convener, AAA 2022 (Mongolia), Ar. Chun Gyu Shin, Vice President, Zone C (South Korea), and Ar. Khurelbaatar Erdenesaikhan, President, Union of Mongolian Architects (UMA) (Mongolia).

Submissions were accepted from April 1 to May 29, 2022, through a dedicated online portal. A total of 268 eligible projects competing under eleven categories were received from twelve countries/regions, which were then reviewed by the jury panel to select winners.

There were 186 submissions from China (174 from Mainland China; twelve from Hong Kong), seventeen from Thailand, fifteen from India, thirteen from Vietnam, eight each from South Korea and Malaysia, six from Sri Lanka, five from Japan, three each from Mongolia and Bangladesh, and two each from Pakistan and Singapore—of these, twenty-four projects were submitted for category A1, ten for A2, thirty-four for B1, twenty-two for B2, thirty-four for B3, sixty-one for B4, twenty-three for B5, seven for C, four for D1, thirty-seven for D2, and twelve for E.

The jury board consisted of Ar. Abu Sayeed M. Ahmed from Bangladesh, President, ARCASIA (head of panel), Ar. Duangrit Bunnag from Thailand (representing Zone B), Ar. Jae Y. Lim from South Korea (representing Zone C), Dr. Ganzorig Erdene from Mongolia (Eminent Nonarchitect Person), and Ar. Erick van Egeraat from the Netherlands (Eminent Architect from a Region Other than ARCASIA).

Over three online panel meetings, twenty-six projects, out of the fifty-eight shortlisted, were selected as winners and awarded commendations that make up nine gold medals and seventeen honorable mentions.

On September 6, 2022, the award presentation ceremony and dinner were held at the Sogombo Hall of the Best Western Premium Hotel, Ulaanbaatar, Mongolia, where ARCASIA Forum 21 was also being held concurrently. During the award ceremony, awards were handed out to the winners or their representatives, with the winning projects exhibited during the day at the Misheel Exhibition Hall, as part of ARCASIA Forum 21's events.

This special issue of *Architecture Asia* is a showcase of ARCASIA Awards for Architecture 2022, and features the twenty-six winning projects from different award categories. We take this opportunity to extend our sincere and heartfelt congratulations to all the winners.

Ar. Abu Sayeed M. Ahmed
President, ARCASIA/Bangladesh

Abu Sayeed M. Ahmed is the dean of the Faculty of Environmental Science and Design at the University of Asia Pacific in Dhaka, Bangladesh. He graduated from Bangladesh University of Engineering and Technology (BUET), Dhaka, and obtained his master's and doctorate degrees in Architecture from University of Karlsruhe (present-day Karlsruhe Institute of Technology), Germany.

He served as the president of the Institute of Architects Bangladesh (2013–2014 and 2015–2016), and president of ARCASIA (Architects Regional Council Asia) from 2022 to 2023.

His professional experience involves architectural work in Dhaka, as well as in Germany, where he was involved in the design of various projects. He is also actively involved in Bangladesh's heritage protection and preservation movement. His conservation related work includes his role as "National Consultant—Architecture" under UNESCO (United Nations Educational, Scientific and Cultural Organization) for capacity building and training for the management of World Heritage sites in Bangladesh. He is currently also engaged in several restoration projects in Bangladesh. He recently received the UNESCO Asia Pacific Heritage Conservation Award.

Ar. Erick van Egeraat
Eminent Architect from a Region Other than ARCASIA/The Netherlands

In his more than forty years of successful practice, Erick van Egeraat has built a highly diverse portfolio containing many ambitious and high-profile projects in the Netherlands, Europe, and the Russian Federation. He has led the realization of over 166 projects in more than ten countries, ranging from buildings for public and commercial use to luxury and social housing projects, as well as projects for mixed use, and master plans for cities, and even entire regions. Each of these projects represents his very personal and expressive vision on architecture and urban development.

Both Van Egeraat and his work have been the recipients of numerous international awards and citations, such as the 2007 RIBA North East Award for Middlesbrough Institute of Modern Art and the Best Animated Architecture Award at the 2014 Media Architecture Biennale for the Waste to Energy plant in Roskilde, Denmark. He was also honored as Knight of the Order Nassau (Ridder in de Orde van Oranje-Nassau) by the king of the Netherlands in 2016.

He graduated from the Department of Architecture at Delft University of Technology, the Netherlands, with an honorable mention in 1984, and was co-founder of Mecanoo, a renowned avant-garde practice. In 1995, he established (EEA) Erick van Egeraat associated architects with offices in Rotterdam (the Netherlands), Moscow (Russia), Budapest (Hungary), London (United Kingdom), and Prague (Czech Republic). In order to better meet the demands of a portfolio as diverse as his, he successfully restructured his company in 2009 into what is now Design Erick van Egeraat.

Ar. Duangrit Bunnag
Eminent Architect, Zone B/Thailand

Duangrit Bunnag graduated from the Architectural Association School of Architecture (AA), London, United Kingdom, in 1995 and has been engaged in his practice Duangrit Bunnag Architect Limited (DBALP) for the last twenty-five years.

Bunnag has received three gold medals from ARCASIA (Architects Regional Council Asia); his accolades over the years include the Wallpaper Designer of the Year Award 2014, ARCASIA Building of the Year Award 2015, the International Architecture Award from The Chicago Athenaeum 2016, and DOTY Most Influential Designer of the Year Award 2019. Bunnag continues to practice and hone "his trade" every day, with his team made up of architects, interior designers, and landscape architects.

DBALP was established in 1998 and has achieved many successes with works that have received awards and recognitions, which include a gold medal in the ARCASIA Awards for Architecture 2015, and "Best Hotel" category winner in the Wallpaper* Design Awards 2014. He has frequently been invited as a speaker and critic for many local and international symposiums, lectures, and events. In 2014, Bunnag renovated the old factory in Bangkok's Khlong San area into a creative art and cultural space called The Jam Factory, which has become a new platform in creative spaces, even spawning other branded projects such as Warehouse 30 and Hotel Bocage.

Ar. Jae Y. Lim
Eminent Architect, Zone C/South Korea

Jae Y. Lim received a Bachelor of Architecture from Seoul National University, South Korea, and a Master of Architecture from the University of Michigan, United States. He established Office of Contemporary Architecture (O.C.A.) in Los Angeles, United States, in 1990, and returned to South Korea in 1996 to establish O.C.A. Seoul.

Lim strives to understand the tendencies of social, economic, and cultural changes in order to reflect them in his architecture through new prototypes. His major projects include his "Evolving Gas Station" series (Hyundai Hydrogen Station at National Assembly, Seoul Oil Corp. Building, Hanyu Group Building, and Yangjae Complex Building), "Ways of Living" series (Duo 302, Junggyebon-dong 104 Village, and Eunpyeong Gija-chon Public Housing), "Factorium: Factory Aesthetics" series (Amore Pacific Beauty Campus Shanghai, Pacific Pharma Healthcare Campus, HK Campus, and Paju Book City FB16), and "Terrafice" series (CLIO Cosmetics and YG-1 Global Head Office).

He has received numerous awards, including a gold medal in ARCASIA Awards for Architecture, a KIA Award, and the grand prize in the Korean Architecture Award. He also served as director of the 2019 Seoul Biennale of Architecture and Urbanism.

Dr. Ganzorig Erdene
Eminent Nonarchitect Person/Mongolia

Dr. Ganzorig Erdene is an associate professor at the Mongolian University of Science and Technology, Mongolia, who has been working in the Structural Engineering Department within the School of Civil Engineering and Architecture since 1984. He attained his bachelor's degree from Mongolian State (National) University of Education, Mongolia. In 1994, he attained PhDs from Moscow University of Civil Engineering, Russia, and Mongolian Technical University (present-day Mongolian University of Science and Technology). He also completed a postgraduate diploma course on Earthquake Engineering at the International Institute of Seismology and Earthquake (IISEE), Japan, from 1996 to 1997.

He has published more than fifty papers in academic periodicals and journals and has been presented at many conferences. He has also supervised the research work of many doctorate and master's students and written many practice codes and standards. As a national registered consulting engineer, he has participated in many foreign-invested and domestic projects. He has been a committee member in many international and national professional societies and institutions, including the steering and award committees of the Asian Civil Engineering Coordinating Council (ACECC), the Mongolian Association of Civil Engineers, and the Mongolian National Academy of Engineering, Science & Technology Council under the ministry. He has also chaired the High-Rise Building Design and Earthquake Engineering Committee in Mongolia. His research focuses on structural engineering, seismic-resistant structures, tall-building structures, seismic capacity evaluation, and the strengthening of structures.

Ar. Batjav Batkhuyag
Convenor, ARCASIA Awards for Architecture 2022/Mongolia

Batjav Batkhuyag graduated from Mongolian State (National) University with a Bachelor of Arts in Architecture in 1979. He also holds a Master of Science in Urban Environmental Management (1997) from Wageningen University & Research (WUR), the Netherlands, and a Master of Architecture (1999) from Mongolian Technical University (present-day Mongolian University of Science and Technology).

Batkhuyag was elected president of the Union of Mongolian Architects (UMA) twice between 2005 to 2009, and served as vice chairman of ARCASIA (Architects Regional Council Asia) Zone C from 2008 to 2010. In recognition of his constant efforts to promote Mongolian architecture abroad and encourage collaborations with overseas architects, Batkhuyag was titled an honorary member of the Japan Institute of Architects (JIA) and the Korea Institute of Registered Architects (KIRA). He has also been honored with awards from UMA and the Union of Architects of Russia.

He worked as head of department of the branch of the local government responsible for architecture and urban development for eleven years, and was also the country facilitator in Mongolia for UNOP (United Nations Office for Partnerships). He has also held managerial positions in the corporate sector in Mongolia, such as Executive Director, S Development LLC, Deputy Director, APU JSC, and General Manager, Bat Daatgal Insurance LLC.

Batkhuyag is actively involved in many public initiatives concerning global climate change, environmental degradation, and sustainable development. He is a founding member of the Mongolian Green Building Council and is currently elected as one of the council's board members.

CONVENER

Ar. Khurelbaatar Erdenesaikhan
President, Union of Mongolian Artists (UMA)/Mongolia

Khurelbaatar Erdenesaikhan has been elected as president of the Union of Mongolian Architects (UMA) three times since 2009, and is currently the ninth president of the union. He has devoted himself to promoting Mongolian architectural and urban development both at home and abroad, successfully leading efforts in many areas, such as improving the education of young architects, enhancing their professional skills and conferring qualification degrees on them, protecting and raising public awareness of architectural monuments, and introducing international standards to the Mongolian National Institute of Architects to promote its international recognition.

He obtained his Master of Architecture from Mongolian University of Science and Technology, Mongolia, and also attended training courses on architecture and urban development in Germany, Japan, Austria, France, South Korea, and the United States.

As a chief architect and the head of the Construction and Urban Development Department in Ulaanbaatar, Mongolia, Erdenesaikhan was responsible for the elaboration of the city development document "Updating the Master Plan for the Development of Ulaanbaatar Until 2020, and the Trends of its Development Until 2030." He has also initiated and led many other big projects.

He has been a member of the Council of the Minister of Construction and Urban Development (Mongolia) for many years, participating in the activities of the working group to develop the "Master Plan for Localization of the Population and the Development of Settlements in Mongolia." Since 2016, he has been the head of the Urban Planning and Architectural Professional Council under the Ministry of Construction and Urban Development of Mongolia, providing professional advice on the design of major projects, industry regulations, and development master plans in the fields of construction, architecture, and urban planning in Mongolia.

He holds the titles "Distinguished Constructor of Mongolia" and "Consulting Architect (City Planning)," and is also an honorary member of the Korea Institute of Registered Architects (KIRA), South Korea. He has been awarded the President's Prize twice, and has also won the Union of Mongolian Architects Award.

As the president of UMA, Erdenesaikhan spearheaded the organization of ARCASIA Forum 21 in Mongolia, and was also convener at that event. The successful forum was held in September 2022 and themed "The Future of Sustainable Urban Development."

Ar. Chun Gyu Shin
Vice President, ARCASIA (Zone C)/South Korea

Chun Gyu Shin is a registered architect with the Korea Institute of Registered Architects (KIRA) and the American Institute of Architects (AIA), and vice president of Zone C, ARCASIA (Architects Regional Council Asia). He is a principal architect and the founder of CGS Architecture and Association in South Korea. He was city architect of Cheongju City, South Korea, and also an adjunct professor at Yonsei University, South Korea, for twenty years.

He completed his bachelor's degree at Yonsei University and attained a Master of Architecture and a Master of Urban Planning from Ohio State University, United States. He was also a member of the Architectural Policy Committee in Seoul's metropolitan government in South Korea, an architectural advisor of Korea International Cooperation Agency (KOICA) (under the Ministry of Foreign Affairs of South Korea), and a master planner of the National Museum Complex of Sejong Administrative City, South Korea.

His notable works include Aimsak Factory—which received a Presidential Award in the Korea Architecture Award 2008 and a gold medal in ARCASIA Awards for Architecture 2010, Chungho Building Remodeling—which received a Seoul Architecture Award in 2008, and Creative Village at Chungkang College of Cultural Industries—which received a Korea Architecture Award in 2010.

SINGLE-FAMILY
RESIDENTIAL PROJECTS

Gold Winner

- Kichul Lee/Architect-K
(South Korea)

Honorable Mention

- Choi Hong Jong
(South Korea)

Grandpa's Cool House

GOLD WINNER

A1 | Single-Family Residential Projects

Award credit: Kichul Lee/Architect-K

Location: Gimhae-si, South Korea

Photography: Joonhwan Yoon

Grandpa's Cool House is a retirement home tailored for the "baby boomer" generation—from years 1953 to 1962—referring to the generation who experienced extreme situations in Korea's modern history, such as the economic development boom during the postwar poverty period; opened democracy against military dictatorship; growing up amid local Korean culture and Confucian values, but in the flow of globalization; and living in the age of capitalist mass culture and global values. This "baby boomer" generation is a multilayered generation that has existed through the many different whirlpools in modern Korean history.

In the course of modernization and industrialization, native traditional Korean architecture has largely disappeared, but still remains a mainstay of Korean architecture. Also, the Western architecture that was newly introduced over the last half century has become a significant part of Korean architecture, especially given changing lifestyles in modern-day Korea. Both these architecture types are strictly independent and exist on the opposite sides in Korean architecture and over time, blended and gone through their own process of natural evolution.

In many respects, the "baby boomer" generation, often referred to as the intergenerational generation, reflects these traits of blending and evolution observed in today's Korean architecture. Against this background, the theme of Grandpa's Cool House is centered on establishing an identity for the "baby boomer" generation and exploring the modernization of native Korean architecture.

Spaces in the building have been organized to add modern functionality and contemporary aesthetics, while maintaining the layout and essence of traditional Korean architecture, which conforms to nature. A traditional *toenmaru* (Korea-style terrace) and *cheoma* (Korean-style eaves) are featured using a corrugated steel sheet and native bamboo, which grows in Gimhae, South Gyeongsang Province, South Korea, to create a modern and natural space. It is hoped that this modern rendition of native Korean architecture that is Grandpa's Cool House will be a space of comfort, like a countryside village, that will serve all aspects of the lives of the unique "baby boomer" generation.

A-MI-JAE

HONORABLE MENTION

A1 | Single-Family Residential Projects

Images

1. East view
2. North view
3. Façade and front yard
4. Terrace on the second floor
5. Entrance to the multi-use room
6. Interior view
7. Living room

Award credit: Choi Hong Jong
Location: Seongnam-si, South Korea
Photography: Kyungsub Shin

This project is located in the residential cluster of NamSeoul Country Club, South Korea. This residential cluster was built over thirty years and all homes here enjoy reliable security that ensures up-to-mark crime prevention that goes well beyond the typical scope of luxury homes. The location of the house, known as Myeongdang—meaning great location in English—befits the overall image of the building and site, which present the appearance of a luxury residence.

The design of the house was inspired by the owner's requirement for a "quiet" house, as well as the look of the site, and recalls an old Korean expression, *Gumeebullu Hwaeebulch* 검이불루, 화이불치, which translates to: "It is simple and humble, but not shabby, and impressive and glamorous, but not extravagant." This expression is often used to describe the culture of the ancient Korean kingdom Baekje (18 BCE to 660 CE) or when comparing the ancient Korean kingdoms Goguryeo (37 BCE to 668 AD) and Silla (57 BCE to 935 AD).

This sentiment of humble glamor is also seen in traditional Korean architectural aesthetics. For example, in Jongmyo Shrine, Seoul, South Korea, in the narrow *toe-kan* (the edge space in a multi-façade house), in between the *taesil* (Placenta Chamber) and *yeolju* (colonnade) of the main hall, there are no ornate *dancheongs* (traditional multicolored decorative paintwork on wooden buildings and artifacts) or sculptures.

Instead, a solemn and sacred atmosphere resides. As another example, the roofs of Haeinsa Temple in Gayasan National Park, South Gyeongsang Province, South Korea, harmonize with the surrounding mountains, striving to attain the highest degree of perfection; and therein lies their elegance.

The previous building on the site tried to add value to its frugal beauty, but that did not come through quite as well. This aspect was, therefore, carefully considered throughout the design process—from appearance to functionality, to modeling, structure, and material utilization, which all also affected the cost of the rebuild. The result translates to a simple mass without decorations, with white stones, continuous elevations of the same scale in all directions, proper internal and external functions, a frame construction with opening to the horizontal, and the careful sizing of each space. The relationship with the street was also considered, also affecting the house's design.

The beginning of the house starts from the 8-meter road on the east side. The yard is located on the southwest side, considering the view and the direction of the house, and on the east side, one volume is placed perpendicular to the road, where the first floor of this volume becomes a parking lot with pilotis. The upper floor is a bedroom mass without openings, and another floating mass is open at a suitable level with the yard.

A2

MULTIFAMILY RESIDENTI
PROJECTS

MoYeoGa

HONORABLE MENTION

A2 | Multifamily Residential Projects

Award credit: Sinwook Oh
Location: Busan, South Korea
Photography: Joonhwan Yoon

Images

1. MoYeoGa within the cityscape
2. Front of residence
3. Back of residence
4. Front of shared room
5. Stairs adjacent to balcony
6. Living room 1
7. Children's room
8. Living room 2

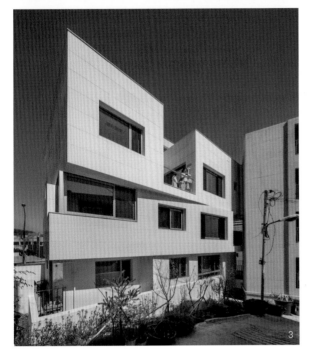

The concept of this home was inspired by a desire to raise children within a community-living environment in the city (instead of the typical isolated apartment-living environment), surrounded by family and friends, to build lasting memories of family, community, and co-living. The project began with two families and grew to include eight, with a total of thirty family members.

This multifamily house is a unique amalgam of living together and having one's own space. MoYeoGa, which translates to "Gathering House," is a home that meets each individual household's budget, as well as family composition and lifestyle, without excessive spending on construction costs, especially with its city center location. It fulfills each family's dream of how they envision a home to be, as well their lifestyle requirements, through focusing on the relationship between exclusive and shared areas, introducing a collection of intermediate and transitional areas. The house also arranges differentiated floor plans, connection points, space compositions, as well as finishings and construction methods

tailored to each household's individual preference—thereby designing the house in part and as a whole.

The closing and opening of spaces are encountered at a natural pace, aided by widened corridors between units that extend the use and function of a typical hallway. The public space is designed as an extension of the private space to allow members of the home to "run into" each other. This is enhanced by visual connections that are established through windows and openings that look out to either private or shared gardens, or passageways. Spatial communication is arranged through terraces, courtyards, balconies, communal yards, decks, a swimming pool, and study room, which can be enjoyed and used easily by every household.

The building of this home has since turned into the creation of a "small town." By sharing their thoughts, day-to-day routines, ins and outs of raising their children, and their way of living, these eight households have become neighbors, friends, and family. The unique traits of MoYeoGa create the possibility of a new residential model in the city for today's Korean society.

B1

PUBLIC AMENITY
COMMERCIAL BUILDINGS

Gold Winner

- Di Ma (China)

Honorable Mentions

- Quansheng Xu and Hao Zhang/ Beijing Institute Architectural Design, OMA (China)

- Danshen Dong, Nong Yin, Zhibin Xiao, Zhoujin Mo, Yuping Wang, Bin Lei, Hanxuan Mao (China)

TMT "Folding Park": Reconstruction of Former Beijing Tuan He Station

GOLD WINNER

B1 | Public Amenity Commercial Buildings

Images

1. The building faces the street with a "soft" spatial model
2. View of lobby from the front yard
3. Bar working area and sky conference room extending toward the inner courtyard
4. The intertwined folding trails in the "folding park"
5. Lobby reception beside the

Within the context of China's urban renewal, this project is an exploration of design that is full of imagination, as well as humanistic considerations. It aims to bring new life to old buildings and also seeks to contribute to the daily life of the city. It also seeks to stimulate the vitality of the community, while also exploring more possibilities in the relationship between architecture and urban life and everyday activities, to bring more public space to the people.

In addition to transforming the old abandoned police station into a new enterprise office building, this project also redefines the "red line" of the site with a three-dimensional "folding park," forming a multilevel open community space between the building and the street. This "red line" between buildings and the street, which was once used to declare and define these specific areas, has now become an open, shared vitality trigger zone, which has greatly activated the vitality of the old urban area.

The "folding park" sets up a series of engaging facilities, such as a swing, slide, punching bag, see-saw, and basketball frame, and connects with the roof park, creating space for a variety of community activities. New facilities can also be "plugged in" to the "folding park" as needed, allowing it grow freely, in tandem with the community's activities and use of it.

The façade of the building is covered with a specular reflective material, which hides its mass and presents the ever-changing reflection of the environment and people's activities as the most vivid expression of the building. This reflective façade also creates the illusion of a wide site and extends the originally cramped space. The interior space of the building has been opened up as much as possible; the vertical traffic is reconstructed and a large number of spaces are embellished with multiple attributes, in order to create as many opportunities as possible for people to meet each other.

Tencent Beijing Headquarters

HONORABLE MENTION

B1 | Public Amenity Commercial Buildings

Award credit: Quansheng Xu and Hao Zhang/Beijing Institute Architectural Design, OMA
Location: Beijing, China
Photography: ArchExist, Xing Fu

Images

1. Bird's-eye view
2. Southeast side of the building
3. West entrance
4. East elevation of the building
5. Staff lobby
6. Roof garden

The new Tencent Beijing Headquarters in Zhongguancun Software Park, Beijing, China, gathers all employees from several buildings across Beijing into this one 334,000-square-meter location.

The new headquarters' volume and holistically arranged flexible internal spaces serve to enhance cohesion and communication among employees working in the building.

The building's design concept is tailored around environmental protection and employee solicitude. Two detached buildings are set in a garden, covering a site area of 7.75 hectares. The main building is designated as the office and R&D facility, while the other is planned as an outbuilding to contain the main building's energy supply. Measuring 36 meters high, the main building has a simple external appearance. This squareshaped floating volume houses seven floors and stretches out horizontally, with an exceptionally large 180-by-180-meter floor plan.

Three entrances are defined by cutting off the bottom corners of the volume's northeast, southeast, and southwest sides. The façade of the building is composed of a standard-unit glass curtain wall, vertical louvers, and a standard-unit metal-plate curtain wall. The main part of the interior space sets the open office area, which is zoned into a three-by-three grid. Each zone is able to function independently with its own core.

UAD Campus in Zitown

HONORABLE MENTION

B1 | Public Amenity Commercial Buildings

Award credit: Danshen Dong, Nong Yin, Zhibin Xiao, Zhoujin Mo, Yuping Wang, Bin Lei, Hanxuan Mao
Location: Hangzhou, China
Photography: Qiang Zhao

Image

1. Three interpenetrating blocks of the building
2. Night view of the building
3. Play of light and shadow in the entrance passageway
4. Interior space
5. Interior atrium

In China's ongoing promotion of the industrialization of architecture, an unconventional rapid construction mode based on prefabricated systems has gradually become a market mainstream. Unfortunately, industrialized constructions are often regarded as being synonymous with un-refinement and inferior quality, thereby calling for well-considered design ideas to truly and effectively express the poetry of architecture in such buildings.

This project focuses on Building 81, one of the buildings in the Zitown headquarters of the Architectural Design & Research Institute of Zhejiang University Co., Ltd (UAD), which was jointly developed by the government of Xihu District in Hangzhou, China, and Zhejiang University in Hangzhou. As one of the demonstrative prefabricated architecture projects selected by the Ministry of Housing and Urban-Rural Development of the People's Republic of China in 2019, this building chalks a prefabricated rate of up to 85 percent and an assembly rate of up to 96.8 percent. It has also been rated as a national Class-3A prefabricated building and a three-star green building.

The key in the design of this building is found in the balance between technology, art, and nature. The building unveils the interpretation of poetic construction: here, architectural design is no longer about purely rational thinking or perceptual output, and any technical decision or creation of perceptual experience is based on both sense and sensibility.

This project shows that rational construction is not constrained by technology, but instead emphasizes the poetry of industrialization, breaking the preconception that the public has about prefabricated architecture as being rough, crude, and cold.

B2

PUBLIC AMENITY RESORT BUILDINGS

Gold Winner

- Pradeep Kodikara,
Jineshi Samaraweera (India)

Honorable Mentions

- Studio Lotus (India)

- Department of Architecture Co., Ltd
(Thailand)

The Kumaon

GOLD WINNER

B2 | Public Amenity Resort Buildings

Images

1. Bird's-eye view of the main building:
   the bamboo-clad dining room
   features views of the Himalayas in

This is a ten-room hotel set in the mystical Himalayan region in Uttarakhand, India. Named after the Kumaon region in the foothills of the Himalayas, this mountain lodge has been designed to respect the environment and celebrate the local culture, with all spaces within enjoying the majestic mountain view.

Established as a base where guests can explore the Kumaon region and learn about Kumaon culture, the hotel is a destination for distinct experiences. This secluded escape set in nature is shaped within a striking but minimalistic architecture. Locally sourced elements weave the hotel's characteristic charm through form—via materials like locally quarried stone, bamboo, and copper—and through substance—by using local crafts such as native woolen fabrics to beautify and personalize interior spaces. Locally sourced recycled wood for the fireplace and rainwater harvesting emphasize the nature-friendly ethos of the hotel and minimize the hotel's carbon footprint to reflect the hotel's respect for and humility toward the magnificent environment surrounding it.

The design vision from the outset was to create a chalet concept, and scatter these chalets around the site, rather than situate accommodation within one big building. Each chalet is conceived as a two-suite unit, with one stacked on top of the other, so as to reduce each chalet's footprint. The chalets (five in total) are then staggered around the site to reflect the contour of the land. Guest facilities are placed on the highest point of the land, within the main building, which also accommodates the library and dining hall. The chalets use local stone as a building material and bamboo as cladding to make the building look light, and feature a terrace (upper suite) and outdoor seating (lower suite) to allow guests to immerse in the indescribable mystical mountain ambiance.

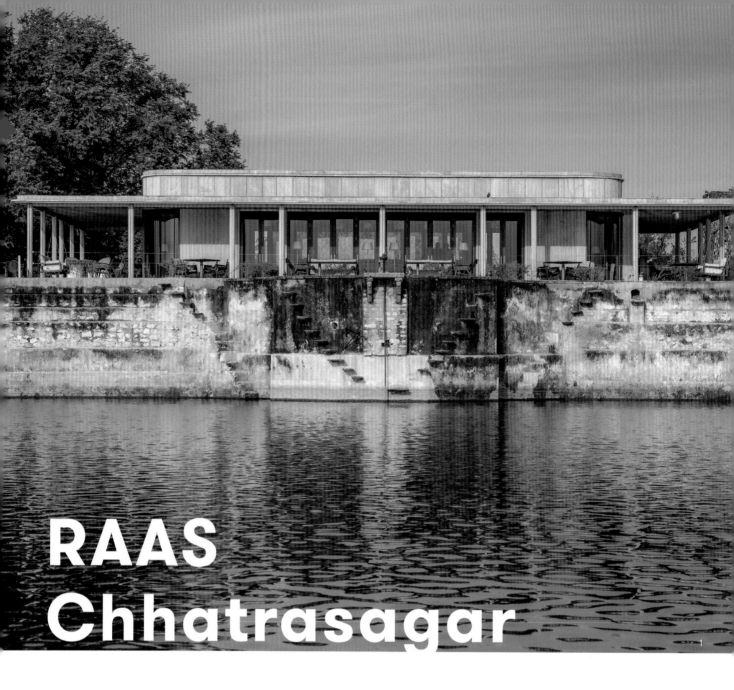

RAAS
Chhatrasagar

HONORABLE MENTION

B2 | Public Amenity Resort Buildings

Award credit: Studio Lotus
Location: Rajasthan, India
Photography: Avesh Gaur, Studio Noughts & Crosses LLP

Images

1. The project is perched atop a nearly 150-year-old check dam that forms a perennial rainwater lake
2. The sixteen tented pods are arranged like conjoined suites
3. Each pod has a continuous tensile fabric canopy for waterproofing and added insulation
4. The softened edges of Baradari, the reception cum bar and restaurant, maximize outdoor vistas
5. The restaurant and reception is edged by an all-season infinity pool to the west
6. A contemporary expression of Rājputana's twelve-pillared pavilion, Baradari's spatial layout is elegant and inviting
7. The interiors feature bespoke furniture fashioned out of locally sourced Acacia (kikar) wood
8. The tented pods are lined with a vibrant canvas that features the diversity of the wildlife in the region

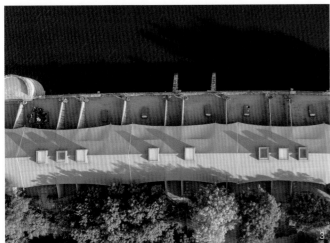

RAAS Chhatrasagar is a sixteen-key eco-hotel perched atop a century-old dam on the banks of the Chhatrasagar Lake in Nimaj, Rajasthan, India, and expands the erstwhile temporary tourist camps set up across the embankment. The lush nature on the property provides guests with a year-round opportunity to observe the region's abundant biodiversity amid 800 acres of pristine forest.

Chhatrasagar Lake is an artificial lake that was formed in the late nineteenth century when a local Rajput noble created an embankment across a tributary to the rain-fed Luni River, with the intent to provide farmers a continuous water supply for irrigation. Replenished by monsoon showers, the reservoir soon transformed the nearby scrubland into a lush arable tract. Over the years, the property mushroomed into a vast stretch of forest, attracting wildlife and native avifauna, as well as migratory bird species. Most farming activities were suspended nearly a couple of decades ago when the owners of the land decided to rewild

the landscape; only a small parcel of the land was reserved for organic farming.

The original tourist camp consisted of an eleven-key tented hotel that was functional only from autumn to the end of winter. During the harsh summer months, it would be disassembled, and reassembled again in autumn. Unfortunately, it also lacked visual and acoustic privacy and offered dismal insulation. The redesign replaces this temporary camp with a perennial property that would be resilient to the region's extreme temperatures, while also increasing the number of units from eleven to sixteen. Public spaces have also been enhanced with a more diverse amenity mix. The sensitive ecological context made it imperative that all additions to the locale be erected with minimal impact. To this end, a system of low-impact foundations and lightweight superstructures were designed, employing a dry construction approach that used lime as a binder in the minimal wet work.

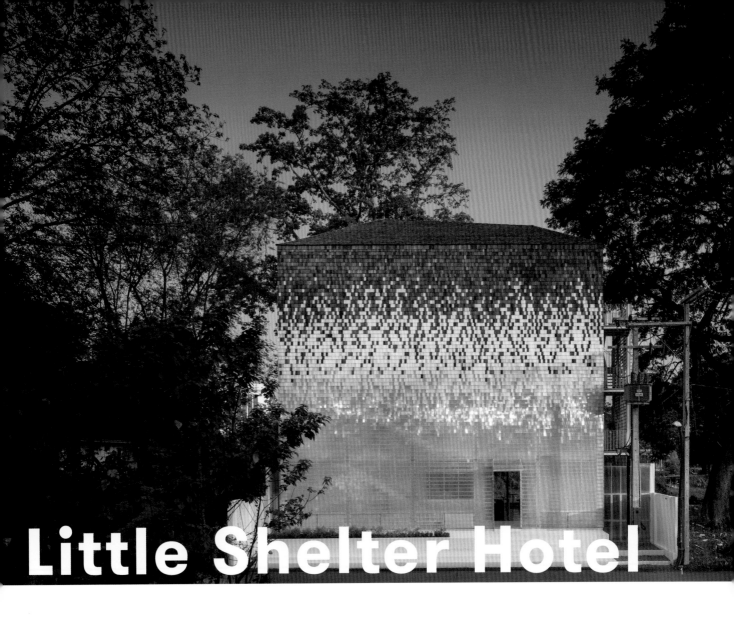

Little Shelter Hotel

HONORABLE MENTION

B2 | Public Amenity Resort Buildings

Images

1. Touched by the morning sun, the entrance façade glitters dazzlingly
2. The roof is partially carved out on the west side to create a roof deck, where guests can enjoy the panoramic river view at sunset
3. The surrounding landscape subtly filters through the translucent architectural surface into the interior spaces
4. A step away from the bright, white lobby, the restaurant/bar is painted n a dark gray, giving it a sophisticated romantic feel
5. The minimalistic lobby and corridor create a gallery-like backdrop to feature at centerstage the 10-meter-high site-specific installation inspired by the famous Boh–Srang umbrella of Chiang Mai, Thailand
6. Images of floating lanterns on the ceiling are infinitely reflected onto two long walls cladded with mirror shingles, creating a surreal borderless ambiance
7. Bright-yellow Boh-Srang umbrellas imbue a fun and vibrant feel to the room
8. An image of Chiang Mai's pine forest on the walls gives the room a mystical mood

Award credit: Department of Architecture Co., Ltd
Location: Chiang Mai, Thailand
Photography: W Workspace

Little Shelter boutique hotel in Chiang Mai, Thailand, samples the region's vernacular architecture, which is characterized by wood structures with shingled roofs. The hotel's roof form, inspired by traditional hip roofs, pays homage to the local architecture of the surrounding old cityscape, with an added asymmetrical form that blends naturally with the surrounding treetop silhouettes.

The west side of the roof is partially carved out to create a roof deck that opens to the panoramic river view. Wood shingles cloak the roof and side façades, and on the river-facing side, polycarbonate sheets cut in the same size as the wood shingles create a striking translucent architectural façade. The entrance façade is marked by solid wood shingles at the top that trickle down into polycarbonate shingles on the lower part, creating a truly eye-catching image.

Even though the exterior design is based on a traditional shingle system, it was possible to achieve an uninterrupted translucent surface through special detail design using translucent studs and special transparent screws. In exploring such unusual design details, the hotel promotes the possibility of fusing new materials with traditional systems to create contemporary architectural finishes that can still be deeply rooted in tradition.

The interior complements the chic exterior with a gallery-like ambiance that appropriately stages installations inspired by the famous Boh-Srang umbrellas of Chiang Mai to create delicate, dramatic silhouettes that express contemporary interpretations of the well-known local handicraft.

The ceiling in each guestroom is adorned with images of iconic venues and landmarks in Chiang Mai. These images are infinitely reflected onto long walls clad with small mirror shingles, creating a surreal borderless sensation. Little Shelter represents an aim to create a contemporary "craft architecture" that embodies Northern Thailand's craft culture. It is not only a place at which to rest your head, but also a representation of the past, the present, and probably the future of Chiang Mai, to all guests who visit.

Terra Center

HONORABLE MENTION

B3 | Public Amenity Institutional Buildings

Award credit: Edward Ng
Location: Kunming, China
Photography: Wang CE/Arch-Radial Images

Images

1. Aerial view
2. Multifunctional public space
3. Semi-outdoor space and backyard
4. Backyard
5. Semi-outdoor space and backyard
6. Multifunctional public space
7. Guestroom

Terra Center is the result of a collaboration between the architects, One University One Village (1U1V) and Kunming University of Science and Technology (KUST), Yunnan Province, China, and it provides an opportunity to improve construction technology and seismic performance of earth constructions in southwest rural China. Located on the university's campus, the center—funded by Chan Cheung Mun Chung Charitable Fund—provides a location to carry out the long-term training of artisans, as well as a space for conducting experiments, research, and practical study. It also enables the reveal and display of technologies and achievements of new seismic earth constructions within a conducive environment, in order to further research and studies.

Integrated with semi-outdoor spaces to provide a comfortable and artistic environment for its users, the center also uses passive design—such as natural daylighting, natural ventilation, thermal mass, and shading—to create an optimal interior climate with low energy consumption. This conscious approach also extends to materials. All the materials used in the walls are natural materials, such as raw earth, gravel, and sand.

No industrial stabilizers, like cement, were added in the earth wall, which is 100 percent recyclable, degradable, and pollution-free. The benefits of these walls are twofold, as results from several mechanical property tests and shaking table tests also corroborate that the seismic performance of the rammed-earth building has been significantly improved, thereby successfully meeting the standards of local seismic codes.

Terra Center is not only a building, but also a research and education tool. Innovative technologies have ensured the safety of the rammed-earth building by improving and enhancing traditional technology with simple materials and tools. Local villagers were employed and trained to build the Terra Center, in the process also leaving them with valuable experience in this area that can potentially convert into a future income stream. The project has also helped to rebuild villager's psychosocial well-being, core values, and sense of belonging. Terra Center presents an appropriated solution for local reconstruction, providing references for national rural construction policies and earth building seismic standards.

B4

PUBLIC AMENITY SOCIAL
AND CULTURAL
BUILDINGS

Nanjing Art Center

GOLD WINNER

B4 | Public Amenity Social and Cultural Buildings

Award credit: Yichen Lu

Location: Nanjing, China

Photography: Qingshan Wu

Images

1. View of the main entrance at dusk
2. View of the art center from the southwest side
3. Exterior and interior
4. View of gallery space
5. View of main stairs
6. View of public corridor

1

Located at the southern end of a new commercial and residential development, the Nanjing Art Center in Nanjing, China, creates a landmark in this new urban development. The design concept iterates a series of linear elements that twist in the section of this two-story volume to combine wall and floor in a single sinuous gesture.

Multiple folded walls encase the building's program and generate an intense spatial richness that creates a series of interlinked public spaces that promote exploration and interaction. The turning and folding of these walls generate experiential richness, connects interior and exterior, and turns the building into a unified form that creates a dynamic presence when seen from the street.

Stone Nest Amphitheatre for Community Activities

HONORABLE MENTION

B4 | Public Amenity Social and Cultural Buildings

Images

1. View of Stone Nest Amphitheatre from bicycle greenway
2. Bird's-eye view of architecture
3. Main access to the stage
4. Stage and grandstand
5. Part of the interior is turned into a café
6. Interior space

Award credit: Wei He, Long Chen
Location: Weihai, China
Photography: Weiqi Jin

This renewal of an abandoned quarry affords an inviting public space to three surrounding villages around the site that are occupied by hundreds of villagers who had been in need of a suitable public venue for events and recreation. Stone Nest Amphitheatre not only improves the environment and landscape, but also adds new buildings and functions that provide a community space to the villagers, such as an outdoor theater and a café. These added facilities also bring new economic benefits to the villages as they provide opportunities to host events such as the local music and drama festivals.

The original stone walls of the quarry are preserved in the design as a background of the stage, to reflect the natural aesthetic of the Orient. The new building conforms to the terrain and embraces the stone walls in an architectural modeling that is simple and rough. The heavy façade exudes a cave-like feeling and responds to the history of the original quarry on the site. The integration of landscape and architecture weaves the architecture into the environment, with steps and ramps on both sides of the building that provide a way for people to enter and exit the stage area. A sloping roof with irregular skylights anchors the relationship between the building and the grandstand, and also strengthens the dramatism of the building's interior, which is set within 280 square meters.

In support of environmental consciousness, local stones are used as the main building material, adding to which natural light and natural ventilation are employed to ensure interior comfort in the building, while reducing energy consumption. The façades were also constructed using traditional stone-laying techniques. The new amphitheater has since become a big part of the community and is highly favored by the locals as a conducive public venue for hosting community activities.

Calm Hill—Spend Time for Living

HONORABLE MENTION

B4 | Public Amenity Social and Cultural Buildings

Award credit: Paul Peng
Location: Beijing, China
Photography: Culture-Mao Disheng, IAPA Pty. Ltd.

Images

1. The east side façade and the rice field leading to it
2. Aerial view
3. View of the building façade from across the river
4. Entrance
5. Courtyard
6. Courtyard and teahouse
7. Leisure area on the second floor

Calm Hill, located at the foot of the Great Wall near Beijing, China, reflects poise and attitude with a serene composure that imparts a vibe of tranquility; almost as if it is "giving time back to life."

An introverted architecture accommodates the compelling geographical location of the site, as an extroverted design demonstrates a "lifestyle attitude" hinged on contemporaneity and flair.

The architect breaks known conventional modes of conveying the information—such as through objects and pictures—and instead tells the story through cultural bonds and the building's interaction with the land. Locally sourced materials, such as charred timber, *mao zhu* (native Chinese bamboo), and schist stone spotlight the local culture of the area and create an environment with rich perspectives and immersive, multisensory experiences; apertures in different dimensions combine to connect people to the various scenes in the space that are displayed in disordered fragments.

The "half" design concept divides the architecture and landscape into two parts, playing on the interaction between the building and the landscape. Each leaves room for the other, but with restraint. Looking back at the building from the middle of the field, the house appears to float on the rice spike. The diagonal wall is a composite strip of openings that provokes people's curiosity, beckoning them back inside to discover more, achieving the home's design intention—where people spontaneously venture outdoors to explore, and return back in to enjoy a well-planned multilevel sensory experience.

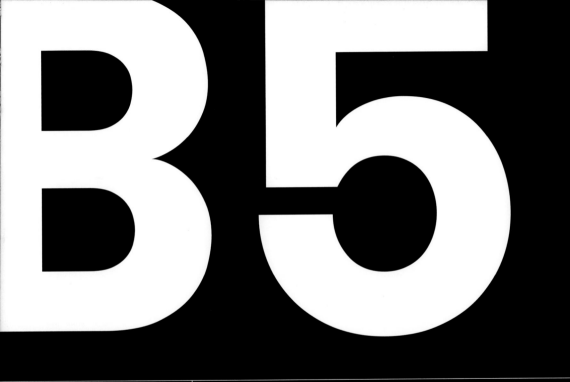

B5

SPECIALIZED BUILDING

Ariake Gymnastics Center

GOLD WINNER

B5 | Specialized Buildings

Award credit: Fujita Kusaba, Hidemichi Takahashi, Masayuki Ishihara
Location: Tokyo, Japan
Photography: Ken' ichi Suzuki, SS Company Limited

Images

1. External concourse connecting to the canal
2. Night view
3. Evening view
4. Interior court connecting the foyer to the concourse outside
5. The arena projects a strong timber note with wooden beams that arc over wooden benches

Ariake Gymnastics Center was designed to function in two phases. The facility's first role was as the venue of Tokyo 2020 (Olympic Games) and Tokyo 2020 Paralympic Games (for gymnastics, rhythmic gymnastics, trampoline, and boccia events), after which it was converted into an exhibition hall following the removal of the spectator stands.

The exhibition hall's design has been tailored to allow for an easy future disassembly, if so required, along the gymnastics center's design emphasis on simplicity—in part also created by a strict budget and construction terms. Despite its modest design attributes, concise budget, and limited building leeway, Ariake Gymnastics Center still shone bright to successfully serve as an iconic expression of Japanese culture and technology, as a central venue for one of the world's largest sporting festivals.

2

Rasulbagh Children's Park

HONORABLE MENTION

B5 | Specialized Buildings

Award credit: Rafiq Azam
Location: Dhaka, Bangladesh
Photography: Asif Salman, City Syntax

Images

1. Bird's-eye view
2. View of the site before renovation
3. Old Dhaka, new twilight
4. View to the north side of the site
5. The lush greenery of the park
6. A celebration of community

Rasulbagh Children's Park is located in Azimpur, Old Dhaka, Bangladesh, a very dense neighborhood with almost 40,000 people living within a half kilometer radius. Over the last thirty years, due to improper maintenance, persistent flooding, illegal occupation, antisocial activities, and vagrancy, the 0.66-acre park (which translates to about 0.066 square meters per capita) not only became a non-functioning site of urban mayhem, but also something of a headache and eyesore for its host community.

The park was one of the thirty-one parks selected for Jol Shobuje Dhaka, a green project launched by Dhaka South City Corporation (DSCC) to revitalize parks and playgrounds, and was one of the most challenging ones to work on. The project was set in motion with the design philosophy, "Trust and Respect," calling for several conversations, meetings, workshops, and presentations with the community before project plans were finalized.

Three major aspects have been addressed with the completion of this project. The first is water management via a new rainwater collection trench that harvests and filters 100,000 liters (which works out to about 250 milliliters per day) of excess water to reroute it—after funneling sewage out—to newly added public facilities and the nearby mosque. The second is community relations to kindle renewed trust and respect among locals. This was spurred by dismantling the north boundary wall and granting round-the-clock accessibility to the park. The newly built promenade, walkways, orchards, and restored playing fields make the park a community courtyard for all. The third is functionality, which has been established by freeing up the disused and illegally occupied veterinary clinic near the park and transforming it into a multipurpose facility with a library, gymnasium, women's club, filter room, councilor's office, rooftop coffee shop, and other inviting facilities. These changes and the collective efforts of those involved in the project have filled the air once again with the musical giggling of children and made this once run-down park a celebration of the community.

INDUSTR

Reforming Duichuan Tea Yard

GOLD WINNER

C | Industrial Buildings

Award credit: Jianxiang He, Ying Jiang
Location: Foshan, China
Photography: Chao Zhang

This renewal project of Duichuan Tea Yard, an old tea mill in Duichuan Village, Guangdong Province, China, involved multiple parties who included two funders (consisting of the project owner who was a local enterprise and the local town government) along with two users (the original tea mill maganerial team and a cultural branding operator), and the architect.

The old tea mill, which was established in the 1950s, had fallen into disrepair as the demand for tea declined in the early twenty-first century. The regeneration of Duichuan Tea Yard consisted of three operations: First, the restoration of tea planting; second, the adding of a stone podium on the periphery of the existing factory; and third, erecting a set of pavilion courtyards on top of the existing buildings.

The stone podium, composed of local black granite, constructs a porous loop that surrounds the three factory buildings. It also redefines the relationship between internal production and natural cultivation, and installs terraces in the new complex. The pavilion courtyards on top, weaved with bamboo and steel frames, interlink the three rooftops into a

whole, creating a leisure and open roof garden that hovers above the surrounding woods. This rooftop courtyard garden connects to the stone podium through corner staircases. The two implanted structures jointly create an organic public domain for staff, tourists, and visitors.

Through the construction of the stone podium, the project redefines the relationship between buildings and agriculture/ nature, while shaping three courtyards within the landscape.

The three buildings of the tea mill are enclosed within these three courtyards. The first courtyard—opening to the main entrance on the west side—functions as a reception and store; the second courtyard is a tea restaurant; and the third and largest courtyard features production workshops, as well as a tea museum on the ground floor. The steel-bamboo roof pavilion courtyards, as an elevated landscape park, offer excellent views to visitors as they overlook the lower stone podium and the landscape. The reform project converts the entire building complex into a three-dimensional eco-production and sightseeing complex that is anchored in a tea island.

Musashino Clean Center

HONORABLE MENTION

C | Industrial Buildings

Award credit: Toshihiro Mizutani, Hiroshi Kimura, KAJIMA DESIGN, Tomoko Fuchigami
Location: Tokyo, Japan
Photography: provided by TOSHIHIRO MIZUTANI ARCHITECTS

Images

1. Musashino Clean Center
2. The philosophy of the project: "A cleaning plant that fits in with the community and is connected to it" creates an architecture that showcases more than just a cleaning plant
3. The facility has a variety of places where citizens and visitors can freely gather and relax
4. A large space renovated from a platform (a delivery route for collection trucks)
5. As you walk around the facility, you can directly observe the entire waste treatment process through large openings
6. The white space connects to the second floor, enhancing the facility's circulation

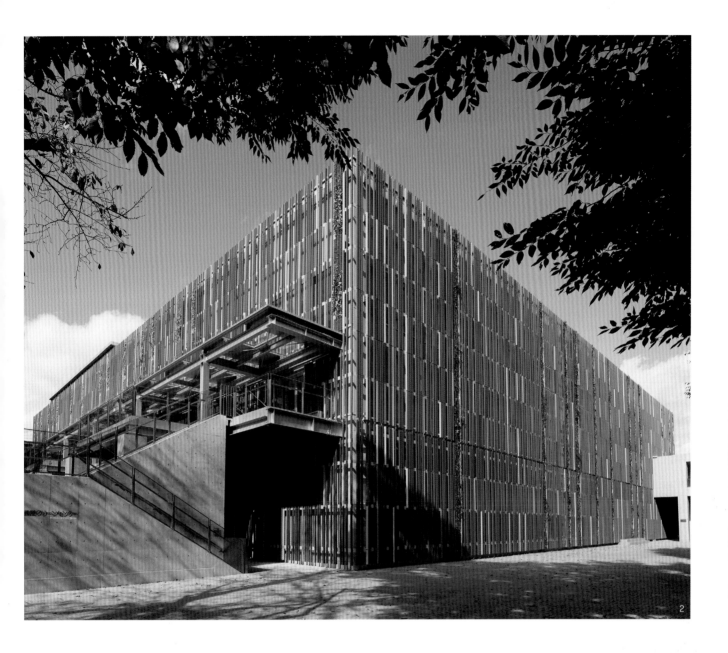

W aste disposal facilities are often attached with strong negative impressions. Generally, people tend to think of them as being a nuisance because of the noise they create and the smells that emanate from them. This project renews Musashino City's thirty-three-year-old waste incineration plant in Tokyo, Japan, to create the new Musashino Clean Center, an open waste treatment eco-facility, where citizens can gather freely and engage in a variety of activities. This new facility aims to create a place that will serve as a base for urban development in the area in an integrated manner, around the main topic of waste disposal.

The facility is situated across City Hall, in the middle of a residential area, which made it essential to ensure consensus among the residents in the surrounding area to allow the project to operate. This turned out to be more challenging than expected due to the Covid epidemic, as people were wary about meeting in person or coming in contact with people. Nevertheless, the design team prevailed and made enough progress to establish a design philosophy to build a facility that operates beyond just a simple cleaning plant; it also highlights social environmental issues using garbage as a prompter. In line with that, the program extends outside basic operational functions to also present Musashino Clean Center as a place where people can engage in a variety of activities that have never before been included in a waste refinement plant.

The building has been designed to look unlike a typical waste incineration plant, with an exterior that harmonizes with the landscape. With part of the building situated underground, it adapts to the scale of the residential neighborhood with ease. Visitors can tour the open treatment facility and observe the waste disposal process, so that they may better grasp the big picture of waste production and its impact on the environment. It also aims to help them understand the significant part humans can play in environmental conservation.

HISTORICAL RESTORATION PROJECTS

Gold Winner

- Chen Ling, Zhiyuan Zhu,
Gang Song, Guanqiu Zhong (China)

Honorable Mention

- AB Concept (Hong Kong, China)

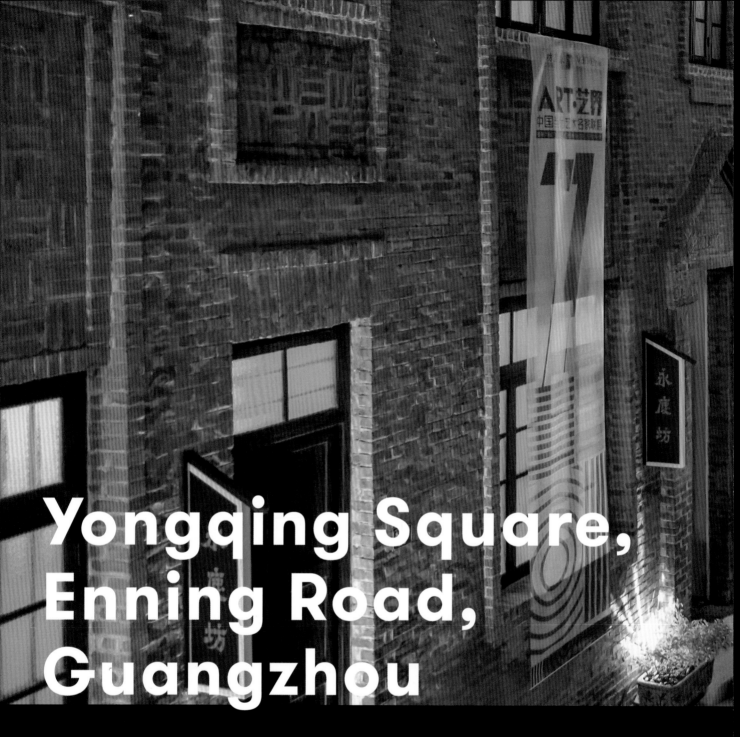

Yongqing Square, Enning Road, Guangzhou

GOLD WINNER

D1 | Historical Restoration Projects

Images

1. Night view of Yongqing Alley
2. After renovation
3. An uncommon standalone building in the square featuring an activity space; shoppers use the stairs along its side as a rest stop
4. Old and new traces interweave
5. The shared courtyard in the co-working office
6. A skylight in the co-working office courtyard funnels in natural light
7. Interaction spaces included to facilitate cultural and social exchanges
8. Bruce Lee's former residence

Award credit: Zhiyuan Zhu, Gang Song, Guanqiu Zhong
Location: Guangzhou, China
Photography: Siming Wu, Ruiyang Tang

1

Enning Road is located in the middle of Xiguan Old Town in Guangzhou, China. As urbanization in the area picked up over the years, the renovation of Enning Road became highly anticipated. However, such renovation was difficult to implement; that is, until 2016, when the developer China Vanke Co., Ltd. transformed Yongqing Square in Enning Road into a multiprogram urban complex.

In the early scheme phase of the project, the architects worked closely with the developer. The developer's resources in real estate ensured that the project would bring back real urban activity and real programs—as many as possible—instead of simply creating just another old town image for tourists.

The heritage of the old houses has been retained and revived by restoring, renovating, and structurally reinforcing them, so that their historical features and accents are restored as faithfully as possible. To complement, elements of transparency, openness, and flexibility have also been introduced, along with "dramatic scenes," to keep up with modern trends and accommodate the needs of today. The old-and-new collisions in this revamp of Yongqing Square make the neighborhood glow with a new spirit. The design reflects an ambitious approach by using small-scale space layouts, original façades, and other traditional approaches, to enable a better, more practical way of revitalizing Yongqing Square. The project has had great public response and has been highly praised by the Guangzhou Bureau of Renewal, and become an example of micro-reconstruction that serves as a valuable reference for old town revitalization in many cities.

Central Police Station at Tai Kwun

HONORABLE MENTION

D1 | Historical Restoration Projects

Award credit: AB Concept
Location: Hong Kong, China
Photography: Owen Raggett

Images

1. The restaurant, named Statement, gives English favorites a local spin
2. The Chinese Library features the rich culinary heritage of Hong Kong's early Chinese migrants
3. Chinese fine dining is elevated with the exquisite décor of The Chinese Library
4. Original elements like colonial wooden shutters blend with contemporary additions in Statement
5. The site's law enforcement past is celebrated at The Dispensary through accents like police badge-shaped mirrors
6. The Dispensary's décor echoes the blue of the uniform of Hong Kong's police force

The former Central Police Station stands as one of the last iconic colonial buildings that depict the rich colonial heritage of Hong Kong. Together with two other monuments in the station compound—the former Central Magistracy and Victoria Prison—it has been revitalized to form the Tai Kwun Cultural Center for Heritage and Arts.

The expansive 7,500-square-foot venue is divided into three areas: To the left is The Chinese Library, a restaurant drawing on the rich culinary heritage of the unique mix of migrants from across China who shaped Hong Kong; to the right, in a nod to the city's colonial past, is a British restaurant named Statement; in the center is a classic lounge bar, The Dispensary, that joins both these venues.

Upon arrival, guests ascend the original grand iron-balustrade stairs, past soaring double-story circular windows, to an ornate reception area on the first floor of the building. Beautifully appointed plaques feature backlit police badges

that remind of the building's history and evoke the atmosphere of the former police headquarters.

In a true East-meets-West fashion, Statement is a British contemporary establishment that pays more than a passing nod to Hong Kong's colonial heritage, but with native influences. The homage to British roots features original colonial windows and frames that add character under wood-framed antique mirrors in the shape of a traditional Chinese plaque. The Chinese Library is a reflection of Hong Kong's local migrant history, which forms Hong Kong's unique culture, with an added dash of Western cultural influence. Linking both Statement and The Chinese Library, The Dispensary is a lounge and bar that pays tribute to the building's law enforcement and authoritarian history. Its winter blue interior, embellished with backlit police badges echoes the uniform color of Hong Kong's police force, keeping the spirit of the building's history alive.

ADAPTIVE REUSE
PROJECTS

Gold Winner

- Lacime Architects
(China)

Honorable Mentions

- Wenqiang Han, Xiaoming Li (Chir

- Chen Wu, Pengyan Ju (China)

- Xinhua Liu, Jinjun Ma, Wei Zhao
(China)

- Hui Wang (China)

SUNAC 1890—Hanyang Iron Works Renovation

GOLD WINNER

D2 | Adaptive Reuse Projects

Award credit: Lacime Architects
Location: Wuhan, China
Photography: Inter-Mountain Images

Images

1. Night view from the street-side
2. Restored inner courtyard
3. Façade restoration of Grade II-listed building
4. Grade III-listed building: the courtyard draws in natural daylight
5. View of the east façade
6. Aerial platform
7. Interior after reconstruction

1

SUNAC 1890, a project that was included in the national industrial heritage list, focused on the renovation of buildings in the factory area of the now defunct Hanyang Iron Works in Wuhan, China. The protection and reuse of industrial sites in such factory areas is important in presenting national industry development, as well as modern industrial culture elements. The two workshop buildings of the project—an oxygen production workshop that is classified as a Grade II-listed listed building and an oxygen charging station that is classified as a Grade III-listed building—incorporated different functions. This led to reconfiguring the buildings' volume and materiality, and also the extent of their preservation and protection.

The oxygen charging station was entirely remodeled due to the ambiguous character of its façade and the low protection necessity assigned to the building. However, its internal structure has been selectively preserved. The oxygen production building, with its red brick façade that breaks for square windows, has been preserved, with the damaged parts in the red brick exterior walls repaired. The ring beams and columns were also leveled with cement mortar.

A new floating corridor has been built between the two workshop buildings and an internal courtyard is now home to old trees from the site that have been retained. By carrying out different levels of preservation and transformation on the two workshop buildings, a new architectural space form has been generated. The brand-new building form is located on one side of Qintai Avenue, with an open front yard that provides a good display area. Upon entering the inner courtyard, one can see the well-preserved oxygen production workshop building, where the side rooms with different heights have been restored to form a complete space. Viewed from the middle of the courtyard, the structure reflects the characteristics of the new era on one side and the spirit of the old workshops on the other, amid trees that are over fifty years old.

Qishe Courtyard

HONORABLE MENTION

D2 | Adaptive Reuse Projects

Award credit: Wenqiang Han, Xiaoming Li
Location: Beijing, China
Photography: Ning Wang, Qingshan Wu

Images

1. Aerial view
2. Front courtyard—night view
3. Middle courtyard—night view
4. Back courtyard
5. Middle courtyard dining room
6. Middle courtyard
7. Back courtyard main bedroom
8. Different building materials complement and belong together

This renovation project is located in a *hutong*-streaked neighborhood in Beijing's Old City; a *hutong* is an alley that is formed by traditional courtyard compounds, known as *siheyuan*, that line either side of the alley.

Measuring 42 meters in length and approximately 15 meters in width, the site occupies an area of nearly 650 square meters. It is a traditional *siheyuan*, which is composed of three courtyards that are enclosed by seven pitched-roof buildings.

The original complex was severely damaged and could no longer be used for dwelling. With the renovation, the client hoped to obtain a quality living environment, and also incorporate suitable public areas for receiving guests.

The buildings needed to mainly accommodate two bedrooms, a living room, dining room, kitchen, tearoom, study, helper's room, storeroom, and an equipment room. A garage big enough to accommodate two cars was also required as the original site did not have one. To ensure good living comfort, the facilities were also upgraded to include water and plumbing channels, and electricity and HVAC systems.

New Shougang High-end Industrial Integrated Service Area, North Section

HONORABLE MENTION

D2 | Adaptive Reuse Projects

Award credit: Chen Wu, Pengyan Ju
Location: Beijing, China
Photography: Di Liu, Chaoying Yang, Beijing Shougang Construction Investment Co., Ltd.

Images

1. Blast furnace No. 3 after renovation
2. Aerial view of the venue for the China International Fair for Trade in Services
3. Night view of Shougang skywalk after renovation
4. Aerial view of Xishi Winter Olympics Plaza
5. Xiu pool
6. The venue for the China International Fair for Trade in Services
7. Shougang skywalk after renovation

New Shougang High-end Industrial Integrated Service Area (Shougang Park) is located in Beijing, China, toward the east of the intersection of the west end of Chang'an Street and the green ecological corridor of Yongding River, covering a total area of 8.63 square kilometers. The project scope covers mainly the north part of the New Shougang area, extending a gross floor area of about 291 hectares, and a total floor area of about 2.27 million square meters; this area has been finished to the utmost quality under the guidance of urban design and style control.

The project oversees the rejuvenation of four aspects of Shougang Park: cultural rejuvenation, industrial rejuvenation, ecological rejuvenation, and vitality rejuvenation. This revitalization project of Shougang Park has achieved encouraging initial results and is on a steady path to realizing the goal of building it into a new landmark in western Beijing.

With this project, the theory of urban regeneration is used to put forward the mode and method of transformation, the development of industrial heritage areas, as well as formulate long-term development strategies and implementation paths. Relevant industrial remains are reconstructed according to the logical framework of "remains detection; value evaluation; accurate design; structural reinforcement; ecological transformation; green construction; operation management." The project has made an active exploration in theoretical innovation, method innovation, and technological innovation, and has achieved extensive international influence in the transformation of large-scale industrial relics. It is hoped Shougang Park will become an important demonstration area for urban revitalization in old industrial areas.

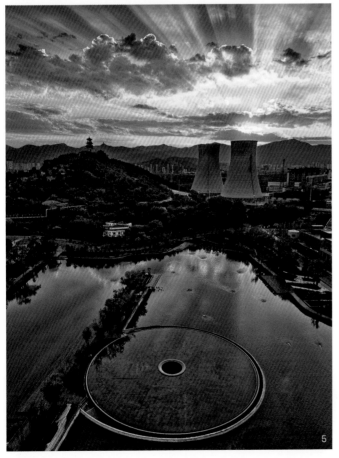

Renovation Project of Shanghai East China Electric Power Building

HONORABLE MENTION

D2 | Adaptive Reuse Projects

Award credit: Xinhua Liu, Jinjun Ma, Wei Zhao
Location: Shanghai, China
Photography: Zhe Zhuang, Wenyi Liu, Yijie Hu

Images

1. View of building's "microwave tower"
2. North elevation—view at night
3. Main entrance
4. Guest rest area
5. Lobby
6. Spiral stairs
7. Suite
8. Rooftop restaurant

Built originally in 1984 to serve as the dispatching and control center of the China Grid Corporation, in 2013 the Shanghai East China Electric Power Building was renovated and transformed into a boutique hotel with new functions to keep up with the trends of the times. The new function plan incorporates facilities designed for a hotel, such as a gymnasium, standard hotel rooms, suites, and restaurant, which are set at different levels according to their function.

The newly built podium covers subsidiary functions like the lobby, reception, and swimming pool. The first floor of the new podium is set back from the control lines, creating street space where tourists can stroll about. The glass boxes on and above the second floor emphasize the lightness and transparency of the architecture with large-scale glass spacers. All the parts that express the unique appearance of the original building are also preserved entirely, such as the

sloping roof, the serrated triangular windows, the "microwave tower," and the facing tiles and window frames on the exterior walls of the tower.

The older elements combined with the hotel's new functions assign a restrained yet distinctive character to the building: for example, the serrated triangular windows are designed to either compose the bright reading and writing space or unique bathroom space. Such design adaptations give the building leverage to follow current trends, even though it is of the past; it is inconspicuous yet luxurious. The hotel not only sits comfortably within its surroundings, but also stands out from it. The amazing contrast between the rustic appearance of the exterior and the delicate space of the interior endows the building with a specific, and whimsically unique, charm.

Xihoudu Relics Holy Fire Park

HONORABLE MENTION

D2 | Adaptive Reuse Projects

Award credit: Hui Wang
Location: Ruicheng County, China
Photography: Baiqiang Cao, Tianpei Zeng

Images

1. Holy Fire Square
2. Aerial view
3. Entrance to the hilltop cave
4. Viewing decks
5. Peeking at the sky through the gap
6. View of the cave
7. Interior of the cave and the acoustic installation
8. Top of the acoustic installation

Listed as one of the national key cultural relic protection areas, Xihoudu, Shanxi Province, China, is a world-class archaeological site that dates back to the Paleolithic Age. Though it is popular because of its link to the Stone Age, little is known of it also being the discovery ground of one of the first uses of fire in human history—which was discovered in the 1960s. The theme of fire has, therefore, always been associated with the site.

In 2016 the Shanxi provincial government built a "holy fire square" for a public torch relay around the province. However, the kitschy design of this square hardly did the reverent, iconic site justice. So, in 2019, the former holy fire square was upgraded to host the flame lighting and kick-off of the torch relay of the Second Youth Games of the People's Republic of China, turning it into a significant venue that is today a part of cultural history.

On the premise of not destroying the original construction, a primitive, mystical, and bold design language was employed to integrate the holy fire square with its natural environment, to create a new space for experiencing the historic, natural site, and to provide a meditation space that is in between the Sacred Mountains and the Yellow River.

The new design was purposed to convert the earlier candidly designed space into a place that is in harmony with the surrounding landscape, and most importantly, fitting of the site's cultural value. The praise received from the live broadcasting of the fire lighting ceremony of the Second Youth Games attests to the success of the new design of Xihoudu. This cultural heritage site has since received extensive public attention and become one of the province's key tourist spots. The new design has encouraged the development of the local tourism economy, promoted the continuous propagation of Xihoudu culture, and also set a model for similar historical preservation projects.

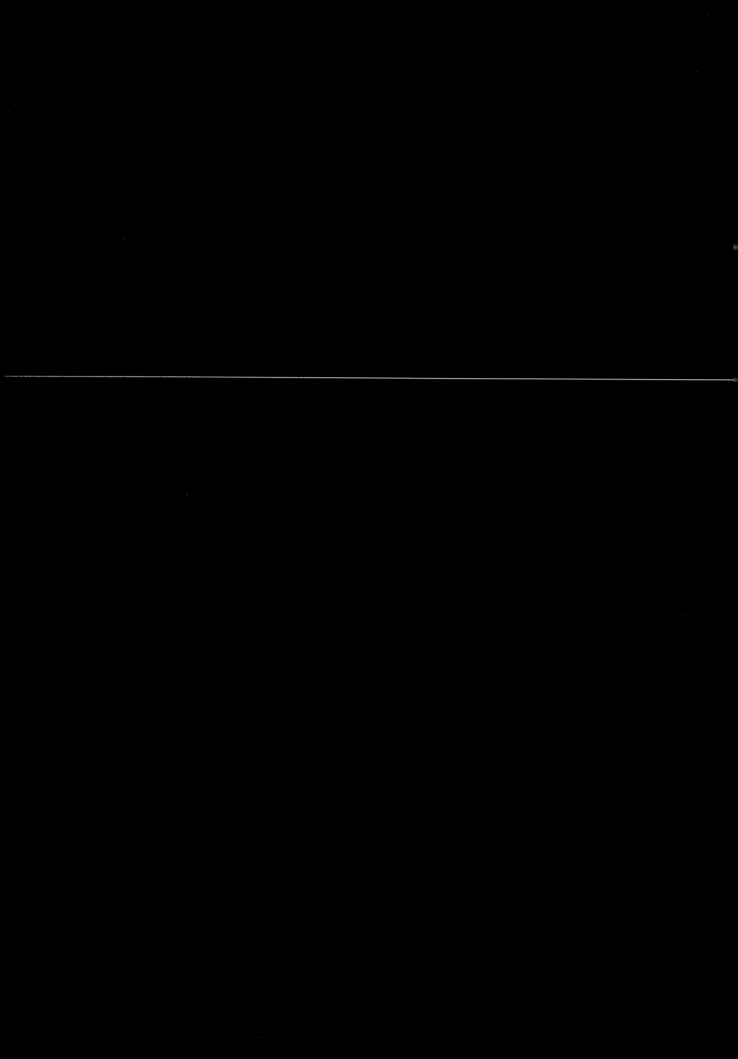

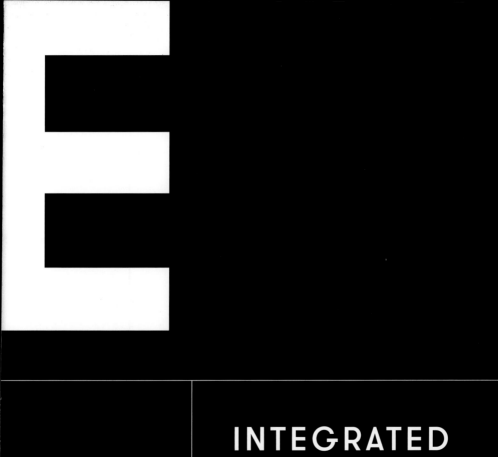

INTEGRATED

Yangshuo
Sugarhouse

GOLD WINNER

E | Integrated Development

Images

The site of this hotel in northeast Guangxi, China, surrounded by the Karst Mountains and the Li River, offers breathtaking natural views. The overall zoning and master planning of this project needed to manage the constraints of space while still enabling privacy—from both a visual and noise aspect—as the size of the site ran the risk of facilities being packed too tightly. An innovative master planning with a low-density development negotiates this challenge by focusing on different zones, guest facilities, spa facilities, and hotel blocks, as well as back-of-house facilities. Employee lodging is also situated away from the site in order to maximize site space.

Due to the proximity of the site to the main road, it was necessary to ensure that the rooms and facilities are well shielded and have privacy. Additionally, there was also a need to ensure that the property would not be disturbed by noise generated from potential sound reflections. On the aspect of visual lines, the elevation of the site maximizes the views received by the suites and public areas. The architectural design and master planning of the structural developments are in full respect of the site topography, geology, and the surrounding natural environments.

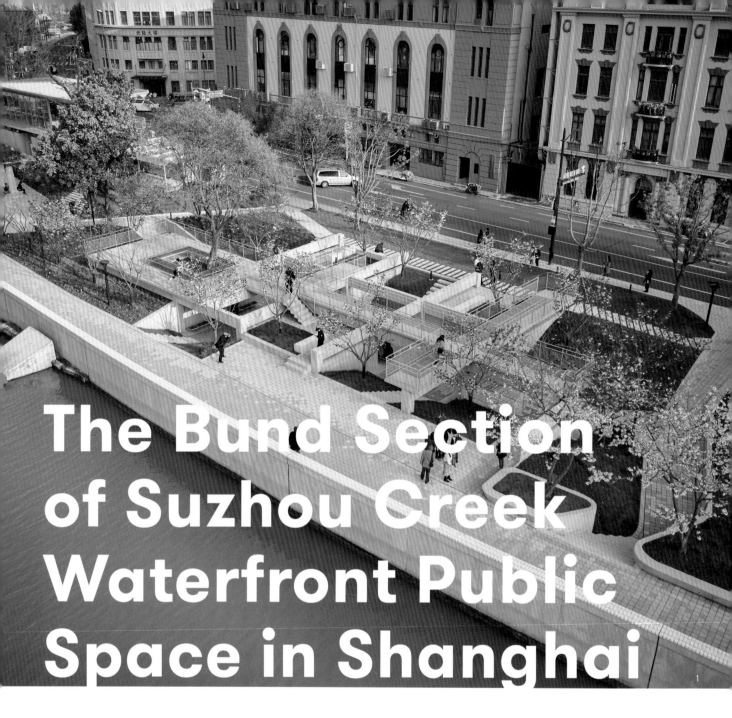

The Bund Section of Suzhou Creek Waterfront Public Space in Shanghai

HONORABLE MENTION

E | Integrated Development

Images

1. Sakura Valley attracts people to the waterfront public space
2. The thoughtful design of the riverfront public space promotes healthy living habits among citizens
3. The welcoming design of the waterfront attracts people of all ages, and a public space for all is created
4. Memories are awakened by a formal reconstruction
5. New urban images are created by integrating new programs with the infrastructure
6. Lightweight steel structure system
7. The Gas Station Café

Award credit: Ming Zhang, Zi Zhang
Location: Shanghai, China
Photography: Yong Zhang

The Suzhou River, as the "mother river" of Shanghai, China, has nurtured the national industry and different varieties of lifestyles in Shanghai for a hundred years. However, accompanying its rich past has also been an unfortunate tragedy, as the river also suffered a serious pollution problem that was generated in tandem with the growth of the city, to eventually became a kind of "back alley of the city." Over two decades of efforts, which began in the 1990s, the river was gradually cleared; today, the spaces surrounding it have been revitalized and transformed into a proud example of a "typical demonstration area for a livable life in a mega city."

The river bund section located in the Huangpu District, at the junction of the Suzhou River and the Huangpu River, has the highest historical concentration and is a core section marked for continual transformation. In the Su Phase 4 project, along the concept "Shanghai's classical times interpreted in a long scroll," this area of the river was transformed from a "gray back side" to an "urban, colorful living room," and has become one of the most exciting waterfront spaces of Shanghai today. In the current post-pandemic era, where encounters and common experiences are more cherished, this historical yet modern, multifaceted yet open, and urban yet natural space will serve as a healing space for people—healing memory, function, and nature—to bring them together. The space will be a place for people to gather, to regain confidence and strength, and to experience familiar feelings of peace and happiness.

TONGJI
ARCHITECTURAL DESIGN
(GROUP) CO., LTD.

Exterior of the TJAD office building

ABOUT TJAD

Tongji Architectural Design (Group) Co., Ltd. (TJAD), formerly known as the Architectural Design and Research Institute of Tongji University, was founded in 1958 and has now developed into a well-known large-scale design and consulting group.

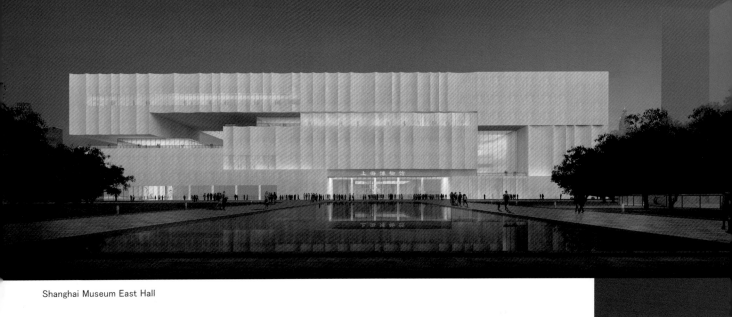

Shanghai Museum East Hall

With almost seventy years of history behind it, and with the profound cultural foundation of Tongji University, TJAD has accumulated a rich experience in both engineering design and technical consultancy, progressing notably over the last sixty-four years. TJAD is a design institution with one of the most extensive design qualifications in China, with a business scope that includes consulting, engineering design, project management, geotechnical engineering, and geological exploration in the fields of building engineering, road engineering, municipal engineering, landscape engineering, environmental pollution prevention, and conservation of historical and cultural relics, among others. The organization has embarked on thousands of projects in China, Africa, and South America that include, among many, Shanghai Tower, Fangfei Garden of the Diaoyutai State Guest House, Table Tennis Gymnasium of the 2008 Olympic Games, African Union Conference Center, New Jinggangshan Revolution Museum, Shanghai Xintiandi, Theme Pavilion of the 2010 Shanghai Expo, Shanghai International Tourist Resort, Shanghai Natural History Museum, Shanghai Symphony Orchestra Concert Hall, China Corporate United Pavilion of Expo 2015 Milan, Havana Hotel of Cuba, Saikang Di Stadium of the Republic of Ghana, the National Arts Center of the Republic of Trinidad and Tobago, Sutong Yangtze River Highway Bridge, and Shanghai A5 (Jiading–Jinshan) Expressway Project.

Shanghai Tower
(Cooperative Design,
in partnership with
Gensler, Cosentini, and
Thornton Tomasetti)

Museum of Art Pudong
(Cooperative Design,
in partnership with
Ateliers Jean Nouvel)

Xi'an International Convention and Exhibition Center (Cooperative Design, in partnership with gmp and WES)

TJAD employs more than five thousand outstanding architectural design and engineering personnel to provide top engineering consulting services for our clients, and we have been working hard to promote urban development, so that we may build a better life for citizens through our many professional practices.

We firmly believe that it is the trust that our clients have in us that gives TJAD opportunities to grow. As part of the society and industry, we strive to continue to channel unremitting efforts toward industry development and social progress, just like we have been doing the past sixty-four years.

Contingency and Temporary Medical Building of Shanghai Public Health Clinical Center

Shangyin Opera House (Cooperative Design, in partnership with Christian de Portzamparc, Xu-Acoustique, and Theater Projects Consultants)

Green Hill, Shanghai

同济设计TJAD

TONGJI ARCHITECTURAL DESIGN (GROUP) CO., LTD., (TJAD)

VISION

Become a respected design and engineering consultancy with global influence

MISSION

Enable people to live and work in a better place with our creative labor

CORE VALUES

Focus on customers and grow together with employees

SPIRIT

Work together and pursue excellence

Address: No.1230 Siping Road, Shanghai, China, 200092

Telephone: 0086-21-65987788

Email: 5wjia@tjad.cn

Web: www.tjad.cn